YO-CAT-067

3 8542 00028 1185

CLINTON TOWNSHIP
PUBLIC LIBRARY
110 S. Elm St., Box 299
Waterman, IL 60556

Plus

Nocturnal
Animals

Fireflies

by Mary R. Dunn

Consulting Editor: Gail Saunders-Smith, PhD

Consultant: Tanya Dewey, PhD
University of Michigan Museum of Zoology

CAPSTONE PRESS
a capstone imprint

Pebble Plus is published by Capstone Press,
1710 Roe Crest Drive, P.O. Box 669, North Mankato, Minnesota 56003.
www.capstonepub.com

Copyright © 2012 by Capstone Press, a Capstone imprint. All rights reserved.
No part of this publication may be reproduced in whole or in part, or stored in a retrieval system, or transmitted in any
form or by any means, electronic, mechanical, photocopying, recording, or otherwise, without written permission of the
publisher. For information regarding permission, write to Capstone Press,
1710 Roe Crest Drive, P.O. Box 669, North Mankato, Minnesota 56003.

Books published by Capstone Press are manufactured with paper
containing at least 10 percent post-consumer waste.

Library of Congress Cataloging-in-Publication Data
Dunn, Mary R.
 Fireflies / by Mary Dunn.
    p. cm.—(Pebble plus. Nocturnal animals.)
 Includes bibliographical references and index.
 Summary: "Simple text and full-color photos explain the habitat, life cycle, range, and behavior of fireflies"—Provided
by publisher.
 ISBN: 978-1-4296-6649-7 (library binding)
 ISBN: 978-1-4296-7120-0 (paperback)
1. Fireflies—Juvenile literature. I. Title.
 QL596.L28D86 2012
 595.76'44—dc22
                          2011001051

Editorial Credits
Lori Shores, editor; Gene Bentdahl, designer; Wanda Winch, media researcher; Laura Manthe, production specialist

Photo Credits
Alamy: B. Mete Uz, 17, 21, Juniors Bildarchiv, 15, Phil Degginger, cover; Getty Images Inc: National Geographic/
Paul A. Zahl, 19; iStockphoto: Andrea Gingerich, 9, Donald Johansson, 13, Joseph Calev, 7; Minden Pictures: Satoshi
Kuribayashi, 5; Shutterstock: Alexey Stiop, 1, Anita Patterston Peppers, 11

Note to Parents and Teachers

The Nocturnal Animals series supports national science standards related to life science.
This book describes and illustrates fireflies. The images support early readers in understanding
the text. The repetition of words and phrases helps early readers learn new words. This book
also introduces early readers to subject-specific vocabulary words, which are defined in the
Glossary section. Early readers may need assistance to read some words and to use the Table
of Contents, Glossary, Read More, Internet Sites, and Index sections of the book.

Printed in the United States of America in North Mankato, Minnesota.
052012
006719R

Table of Contents

Blinky Beetles

At night, fireflies rise

from bushes and grass.

These nocturnal beetles

blink their lights

in the darkness.

5

About 2,000 kinds of fireflies
live around the world.
They live everywhere
except cold polar areas.

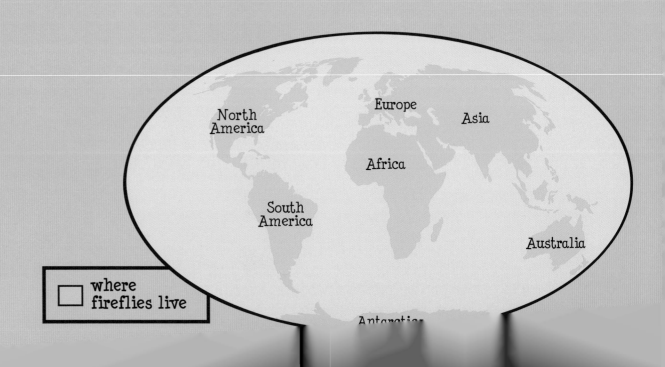

where
fireflies live

North
America

Europe

Asia

Africa

South
America

Australia

Antarctica

Up Close!

Fireflies have brown-black

wings and six legs.

Their bodies are less than

1 inch (2.5 centimeters) long.

CLINTON TOWNSHIP
PUBLIC LIBRARY
110 S. Elm St., Box 298
Waterman, IL 60556

CLINTON TOWNSHIP
PUBLIC LIBRARY
110 S. Elm St. Box 299
Waterman, IL 60556

9

Fireflies have chemicals

in their bellies

that make light.

Each kind of firefly blinks

in a different way.

Finding Food

Some kinds of adult fireflies

eat nectar or pollen.

Other adult fireflies

do not eat at all.

Growing Up

Most female fireflies lay eggs

in soft, wet dirt.

Others lay eggs in trees or grass.

Larvae hatch from the eggs

and burrow into the ground.

Larvae gobble worms and slugs

for one to two years.

Then they change to pupae.

Finally, they grow wings

and become adult fireflies.

Staying Safe

Frogs, birds, and spiders
eat fireflies.

To stay safe, fireflies
hide in bushes
and tall grass.

When in danger, male fireflies

ooze a chemical.

The nasty smell and taste

keep enemies away.

Glossary

beetle—an insect with one pair of hard wings and one pair of soft wings

burrow—to dig a hole or tunnel underground

chemical—a substance that creates a reaction

hatch—to break out of an egg

larva—an insect at the stage of development between an egg and a pupa when it looks like a worm; more than one larva are larvae

nectar—a sweet liquid found in many flowers

nocturnal—active at night

polar—having to do with the icy areas around the North or South pole

pollen—tiny grains that flowers produce

pupa—an insect at the stage of development between a larva and an adult; more than one pupa are pupae

Read More

Hudak, Heather C., editor. *Fireflies.* World of Wonder. New York: Weigl Publishers, 2009.

Rau, Dana Meachen. *Flash, Firefly, Flash!* Go, Critter, Go! New York: Marshall Cavendish Benchmark, 2008.

Trueit, Trudi Strain. *Beetles.* Creepy Critters. New York: Marshall Cavendish Benchmark, 2010.

Internet Sites

FactHound offers a safe, fun way to find Internet sites related to this book. All of the sites on FactHound have been researched by our staff.

Here's all you do:

Visit *www.facthound.com*

Type in this code: 9781429666497

Check out projects, games and lots more at **www.capstonekids.com**

CLINTON TOWNSHIP
PUBLIC LIBRARY
110 S. Elm St., Box 299
Waterman, IL 60556

Index

Word Count: 166

Grade: 1

Early-Intervention Level: 14